T0128232

THE RESPONSIBILITY
OF MANHOOD

JEFFREY BERNARD BOWENS AS, BS, MSM

Order this book online at www.trafford.com
or email orders@trafford.com

Most Trafford titles are also available at major online book retailers.

Print information available on the last page.

ISBN: 978-1-4907-9684-0 (sc)
ISBN: 978-1-4907-9685-7 (e)

Trafford rev. 08/28/2019

 www.trafford.com

North America & international
toll-free: 1 888 232 4444 (USA & Canada)
fax: 812 355 4082

Dedication

This is dedicated to my parents Elisha and Agnes Bowens. My parents distilled in me early in life the importance of GOD and Manhood. GOD along with my mother and father developed me into being the man I have become today. My parents would always say that with GOD in my life everything is possible. I think about my life growing up in Eufaula Alabama, and I have so much to be thankful for. I want to first give thanks to GOD for all the spiritual blessings he has given me. I am just so grateful for all the blessings in my life. I am thankful for my family who continues to give me unconditional and genuine love.

The purpose of this book is to help men find direction in life. To serve as a guide to the young men who do not have a father figure in their life. When we are not careful, we may take the wrong turn in life. The wrong turn could be the difference between life, death, failure, or success. We follow a day by day journey praying to strengthen our relationship with GOD. Men are created in the image of GOD. Sometimes as men we seem to forget what is important. What is important is our health, family, and fatherhood. GOD wants us to believe in him and serve while helping others believe in him. So many people are in doubt and have given up on their dreams. The life they have lived and the things that happen around them cause them to lose faith. We must have faith even when it seems that what we are seeking is impossible. So many people miss out on their dreams because they don't have faith. We are images of GOD and through him everything is possible. Never believe there is something in life you can't accomplish. Our values and accomplishments in life set the direction for young boys growing up. Boys model themselves after their fathers. What they see their fathers do is what helps develop their manhood. For example, if the father is loving, supportive, and kind around the boy then the behavior will be recognized, and the boy usually models the same behavior.

We pray for GOD to give us the strength to make the right decisions. We pray so that as men although we are not perfect can set a good example for young men. Finally, we pray for changes to occur in our lives so we can develop a relationship with GOD. Men are supposed to provide and protect the family. Today's men are not playing their roles as fathers and husbands. So many men feel they are not doing what is expected of them because of the society. Times have changed, and life is a lot more difficult to live. If you don't run into difficult obstacles, then you won't learn anything. The brain must be unlocked and the more you learn the more knowledge you possess. Remember never put a limitation on how far you can go in life because through hard work you can accomplish great things. For example, the soul is as important to a body as DNA is to a cell. Without the soul, the body will not function; just as a cell cannot function without DNA. Remember that through GOD we can do all things, and he is always on our side. Never doubt yourself in any circumstance because you are a child of GOD.

A shift in society has made living difficult for many men. We can't settle for just any kind of job you have to build a strong foundation. The old times where women stay at home and cook have changed. Young men need to attend college and major in something they are passionate about. Next, graduate with a professional degree it may take years but it pays off at the end. It gives you time to develop your manhood as well as prepare to be able to take care of a family. Don't be afraid to welcome change. Many men of today make the mistake of thinking old fashion; however, the old standards are not accepted by the women of today. The women of today want to be financially covered, secure, and treated with respect. Men respect your wife remember she is a representation of you. Hold the door open for her when she enters and leaves with you. Remove her coat and pull out her chair when she intends to sit. Fathers your sons observe what you do daily, and if the father shows no respect towards his wife the son will probably do the same to his wife. My Father distilled in me the importance of being a man and having respect for my wife, and that through GOD everything is possible. Watching my father opening and closing doors for my mother and reminding her how beautiful she was each day made her smile. It made me happy to see this type of behavior.

Perseverance is when someone refuses to give up or let go of something. Perseverance is the ability to keep moving regardless of the circumstances. You press on even when you feel like quitting. Perseverance allows one to act even if they are not motivated. Perseverance leads to success in life. Yes, sometimes you may stumble and fall but GOD will lift you back up. Having a good imagination also helps when it comes to perseverance. When you dream about your future don't let one failure in your journey to success dictate the rest of your life. Drive thru the bad days because your good days will surely outweigh them. Perseverance is important when trying to live a good life you can enjoy and be very proud of. The absence of perseverance will keep you from getting far in life. When you're in your math class and you have a problem maybe you forgot a step, or you added or divided the wrong number. For example, in college as a freshman you must be disciplined enough to do your assignments without someone reminding you. Don't give up remember that if you persevere and pray GOD will help you find the answer. In order to persevere in your toughest and most challenging time you must pray and have faith.

Self-discipline is a necessity in every area of life, and although many people understand its importance only a small few attempts to strengthen it. Self-discipline is the combination of having self-control, using one's common sense and inner strength. Self-discipline gives you the courage to succeed by never quitting. To rise above challenges and problems on the road to success and achievement you must be persistent which requires self-discipline. People who lack self-discipline fail and never reach their dream. When someone discovers self-discipline, they are ready for the hard life ahead of them. There will be both good days and bad days, but you must be disciplined enough to except them both. The more self-discipline you are the more confident you become, and the more confident you become, decreases the chances of doubting yourself. When you unlock the potential you then you can move on to bigger things in life. The bible states that if we are faithful to GOD and confess our sins, we will be cleansed and forgiven. If we continue to pray and grow spiritual, we will be able to accelerate forward and achieve great things in life. Life can knock you down to your knees. What matters next is we must find the strength to get off our knees and keep moving forward. We must understand that we must have the will to never quit regardless of the obstacles. When you stay in the past you never move forward to see what the present has to offer. You must be discipline enough to choose right over wrong.

A young man left home in the summer of 1993 to go off to warrant officer school for the Army. He had spent time in ROTC during college which prepared him in some areas of becoming a warrant officer. The school was in Fort Rucker Alabama. The school instructors made life very difficult and required a lot of reading outside of his daily duties. During the day the young man was learning how to lead as well as overcome challenging obstacles. He had seven weeks to complete everything, but he didn't give up. He had some sleepless nights, but he kept on doing what was required of him. The young man would pray each night to ask GOD for the strength to succeed. He understood that he could not accomplish this alone. Prayer changed his mind set concerning the school. The young man became more motivated. The young man was self-disciplined enough to keep moving forward even when others couldn't overcome the obstacle. The result was the young man graduating from warrant officer school as a chief warrant officer II.

I was always taught that it's not where you come from but where you are going in life. I always wanted to go to college after high school, so I attended college and never looked back. Then shortly afterwards I attended graduate school and earned my Master of Science degree in Management to further my professional development. I would not have been able to do any of this without the grace of GOD. GOD's purpose for everyone differs from person to person. For young men to construct knowledge, they need the opportunity to discover for themselves and practice skills in real situations. Self-discovery is having the opportunity to study things that are meaningful and relevant to one's life and interests. For example, a teacher teaching a class will need to understand that all students do not reciprocate information the same. Developing a curriculum around a young man's interests motivates and stimulates the passion about the lessons of study. When you give boys opportunities, they can generate ideas and set goals for the future. When boys have ownership in the situation, they are motivated to work hard and acquire skills necessary to reach their goals. Father and son talks are one way to encourage such dialogue. I believe young men have greater respect for their teachers, their peers, and the lessons presented when they feel safe and sure of what is expected of them. I feel there is a need for compassionate, strong, and dedicated individuals who are excited about working with children. In our competitive society it is important for young men to work with someone who is aware and sensitive to their individual needs.

We must all learn how to build trust within relationships. So many relationships are full of problems because there is a lack of trust. Husbands and wives must trust each other in order to have a healthy relationship. It can take years to build up trust and only a second to destroy it. Our GOD will not let us fail because each obstacle we get through the closer we get to success. The difficult world we live in makes it hard to really know who you can trust. If everything we wanted in life was easy to achieve then we would never learn anything. Trust is something that keeps the fire burning between husband and wife. When you feel like you are losing trust, and all is lost remember

GOD is still in charge. We must start believing in GOD and thank him for our blessings before they happen. You must have faith which involves relying on GOD and believing with your heart anything is possible. Remember when life is not going good remember your good days. Christ came in the world to save us because we were sinners. We all have sinned but when we ask GOD to forgive, he will. We were born into this world, but we are not perfect. Jesus is the only man that I know was perfect. The Lord expects for us to minister to others to help save souls. We serve a mighty GOD who can do all things so we should never be afraid to worship. There are so many children that have lost trust because of life changes. Trust in Jesus when life is at its worst, Jesus is the way and the light. When you confess to GOD it is like you have a new start. For example, when you are squatting heavy weight your back feels as if it is going to give out. This represents all the sin you are carrying around. When you confess to GOD your sins are forgiven and that heavy load is gone.

Why is it so hard for us to forgive? We all make mistakes, and no one is perfect. Forgiveness is necessary because if you can't forgive others GOD will not forgive you. If someone hurt you in the past you should not hold on to that hurt. The past means it already happened and you can't go back and change it. No man or women is perfect, so we are all born to make mistakes. While we are busy not forgiving, we fail to see what the present has to offer. The choices we make in life can take you very far. There is a right and wrong choice. GOD expects for us to follow his commandments and make the right choices in life. Sometimes we expect GOD to give us certain things in life before we are ready. GOD must sometimes take us through another obstacle, so we are better prepared for what we ask for. Some things we ask for we never receive because GOD understands what we need. If we never go through the obstacles, we want to be strong enough to succeed. GOD prepares us to endure situations even when we are tempted beyond our abilities. For example, a paralegal must complete the requirements to be a paralegal first. Once the paralegal has learned enough to move forward there are other obstacles in place to become a Lawyer or Judge. GOD must prepare us for what is still to come. GOD has a purpose for all of us and all we must do is ask for his guidance. He may not come when we desire but he is always on time. GOD made man in his image and he can do all things. Which means we can also do all things through Christ.

Being a leader in life are shoes that not everyone can fill. GOD put men here to be leaders over their family. GOD can help you be a faithful leader by serving him and believe that Christ died on the cross for us. Christ is the greatest example of a leader. The individual who leads will need to be the kind to lead by example. For example, if the wife is better at managing money than the husband it makes more sense for her to handle the finances. See the leader must be able to make the best decision. In order to make the right decision we must learn to be followers before we can lead. Lack of leadership today by the husband is one of the biggest problems of today. Some didn't have a father figure to look up to so moving from a boy to manhood can be a problem. This is also because many fathers are not around during their son's life. Too many women are forced to act as fathers and mothers. GOD has ordained men for the role of leadership however so many men do not know how to lead. Adults do not always provide a good example of leadership for the young generation to follow. It has become a confusing struggle for the young and we as men have got to accept our role. We have a role in the church and in society to help save souls. Spiritual leadership is about bringing people to GOD. People come to church and receive a message and relate the message to themselves. Monday morning comes and they easily forget and go back to doing the same things again. We see so many people each Sunday that just sit in the church and never shout out for the lord. Yet the same individuals show up at a football game and shout until no end. How can they praise a football game more than the lord? GOD is second to known and we should never be slow to praise him. Men must have a kind heart towards everyone, and we cannot discriminate because someone is different. Men must be accountable within the body of Christ for dynamic growth to be present. The church represents the body of Christ and as men we must bring in others so they can worship. Men must edify people so they can understand the importance of serving

GOD. It is important for us as men to possess spiritual leadership. This will keep us on the right side of the mountain. GOD knows when you doubt him. We must keep faith and never complain when he doesn't answer when we want him to. GOD is always on time and he is never late. You don't have to ever doubt the Lord. Men we should always have faith and believe that there is nothing wrong with claiming things ahead of time. Faith is having confidence and believing in the heart what you want will happen. A little lesson about doubt is that it will always keep you from achieving what you deserve.

The dreams we grow up having will never occur if we haven't enough faith. For example, if you want to go to Harvard to medical school you should claim it ahead of time. Remember GOD is always the reason for the season. Faith is the root to Christianity and if you don't have faith you are not a Christian. Men satisfy GOD by showing they have faith and by being righteous. Praying and talking to GOD without faith will keep you from having a happy and joyous life. We must understand that GOD has done enough for us all to never doubt him. GOD's faithful promise was fulfilled when Jesus died on the cross for our sins. If we repent and accept Jesus Christ, we will be forgiven for our sins. GOD will not accept unfaithfulness and he is a jealous GOD. If we continue to study the word of GOD and believe in our hearts we shall be saved. People in unfaithful relationships are miserable and will fail to survive the obstacles to come. Husbands and wives are one and should always remember they love each other. We as men learn to trust GOD by studying his word and reviewing the things he does in our lives. Remember we are in this cruel world and trust and belief in GOD is the only way to survive. When the days seem to get worst that is when we need GOD the most. When the challenges we face seem to be impossible to cross we still must have faith in our GOD. Some challenges we must cross are necessary for us to be prepared for what comes later. You don't walk and then crawl you learn to crawl first then small steps before you walk. Faithfulness to GOD gives us great peace and assurance. GOD promises us the reward of eternal life in Heaven.

Obstacles are barriers in our life we must cross. Crossing the obstacle is not easy and can sometimes seem impossible. Problems come in our lives daily and the closer we are to GOD the more obstacles we face. This is because satin comes to keep us down and away from the good in our lives. We must endure and stand up to the challenge because in the end we will only be stronger. We are better prepared when we face the obstacles, we face daily such as the boss at work, the enemy against us, and satin. Our thoughts and emotions are our obstacles. The way we think and react can influence the outcome of defeat or success. Defeat will keep you from reaching your purpose in life. For example, when my father and grandfather died, I had to face the obstacles in life due to actual experiences. When I had them in my life their motivational conversations and mentoring help me overcome many obstacles. What doesn't kill you will only make you stronger and wiser. Remember obstacles are designed to keep you from reaching your full potential in life. Jesus died for our sins so that we could be saved. We must learn to come to Jesus and repent. We should never be ashamed to repent and confess our sins. Jesus had mercy on us when he died on the cross and we all were in hell. Our sins are washed away through repentance. For example, a married couple having problems in the relationship should repent. Sometimes running to the marriage counselors has no effect on the relationship. Sometimes couples need to turn to GOD and have faith. If the couple repents and forgives the hurt and arguments can be replaced with a marriage of peace and happiness. We are not perfect and sometimes we treat others in a way they do not deserve. Whether it is the wife, children, or friends we must strive to be more like Jesus. Men you must repent before GOD will forgive your sins. Once we repent, we must be careful not to fall back into sin. We do this by praying to GOD to make the necessary change in our lives to be a better man.

What do you do in hard times when it seems you have nowhere to turn? Do you just give up and throw in the towel or continue to have faith? Some will give up and never go any further in life because giving up is so much easier to do. They will never reach their purpose in life. We are all born to do a specific task, but we must not give up in hard times in order to arrive to our destiny. You should remain obedient and believe that the Lord will make a way out of no way. He always has and always will. Remember he is a way maker when we can't make a way. It doesn't matter how bad the storm is you are going through remember faith will give you peace. The storms we go through are designed to strengthen you. When everything is bad, we must continue to pray and believe that GOD is with us. GOD will never leave you although sometimes it seems you are alone; he is always there watching over you. My grandfather would always say that "although we have troubles in this life there is no comparison to eternal life in heaven". He was saying that we will have bad days and weary days, but if we endure them in heaven we will have to worry no more.

Prayer is a powerful thing and when we pray to GOD, we see spiritual miracles day by day. Pray each night before you lie down to sleep and thank GOD for allowing you to make it through the day. Pray in the morning when you awake from a good night sleep and thank the lord for allowing you to see another day. Remember tomorrow is not promised we are here because of GOD's grace and mercy. Pray will change a person from the inside and provide communion with GOD. Praying to GOD will increase our ability to understand him. If we pray enough, we will learn GOD's character and plans he has for our lives. Prayer is the responsibility of everyone and with it we can change circumstances and situations. There are always barriers which slow down our walk with GOD, but prayer allows us to overcome and overthrow the enemy. The enemy is always trying to change your level of thinking and without prayer he will succeed. GOD has answered many prayers in my lifetime growing up, and I have witnessed many miracles. If people really understood how powerful prayer is, they would pray more. So many people do not pray but prayer is a powerful weapon which we can use to fight our battles and tell GOD what we need. Spending time to get spiritually educated is very important for every man. We are the leaders that are responsible for our families. GOD made us in his image not to remain boys but to grow up and be men. The closer to GOD the family man is the better he will be at leading his family the spiritual way. If a boy was raised in the church working every Sunday being taught to serve GOD. Because of the culture distilled in him to serve the LORD for so many years he will understand his purpose. Spiritually educated means you are wise enough to understand that a relationship with GOD is very necessary.

GOD gives us time to read his word to understand for ourselves. The more we read the bible the more we understand how to deal with the world we live in. Reading will give you direction when you are lost, and you feel like you are not going to make it. It informs you that GOD is still by your side even if he doesn't respond when you want him to. Remember GOD is never late and is always on time we just must ask, and we shall receive. Have you ever been told to keep your nose out of another people's business? Well this is a statement that involves worrying about your own affairs. For instance, if you are busy worrying about what someone else is doing in life, you will not see what you are missing in your life. As Christians we should not be nosy and don't put your input in matters that don't concern you. We are all sometimes fooled to believe that everyone is for you or everyone is on your side. We must understand that everyone is not wishing you well and hoping you will succeed because we live in a jealous and cruel world. People sometimes want to know your business not to help, but just to know it and have something to gossip about. Some feel if you are not making six figures and riding around in new car you are not on their level.

Some people try to get close to you because of what they feel they can get out of you. You will understand that what you have is not because of your college degrees but it is all because of the grace of GOD. A small Church in Alabama about 3000 square foot was being built in small area. The old church had to be rebuilt because it had been there for many years. The congregation was only a head count of about 40 people, but they had much faith in GOD. The deacon was determined to get the new church up before moving out of the old church. The deacon faced many obstacles each time such as land permits, loans denials, and cemetery space. The deacon kept his faith in GOD. He had to build around the cemetery because space was limited. Finally, the parking area was not large enough, and everyone would be parking their vehicle close to the highway. The deacon had faith things would change and GOD made a way. There was about 1 acre of pine trees behind the church, and the deacon was approached by a pulp wood company about cutting the timber. He agreed and this opened a larger area for parking and a larger cemetery. The deacon kept his faith and everything changed. The deacon kept his faith, and everything changed. You can't have mountain moving faith by having a little faith. If we are convinced that we have small faith, we will live and function as if our faith is small. However, when we change the way we think concerning our faith, we will witness Gods mountain moving faith. We are sometimes faced with decisions we are not ready to make. The decision that will change everything including our faith. We understand that what we hope for is not always what GOD allows us to have. We must be spiritually educated enough to understand that GOD will always do what's for the better past what eyes can see. We must have the patience to wait until we hear the voice of GOD telling us to move. Sometimes GOD will ask us to take small steps to get ready for what is still to come. We miss our blessing sometimes because of small things GOD requests from us that we take for granted.

For example, if you are asked to participate in church as an usher, member of the choir, or simply taking up offering, do it with dignity. We sometimes do things that don't involve us in life. What we do can give our young boys and girls a guide as to what working for GOD means. GOD doesn't just want us to come and hear a word on Sunday morning. He wants us to serve him and be workers, try to save others that need saving and uplift others spiritually and intellectually. Encourage others, share your spiritual knowledge and stay humble for our GOD is a great GOD.

We continue in life to do everything except serve GOD. We go to work but not church and we read many books but not our bible. Church represents the body of Christ and the Bible represents the word. We must be obedient not doing so is why our blessings we are to receive are delayed. We make many excuses as to why we don't work in the church or why we don't go to church. Spiritual growth is not possible without developing a relationship with GOD. Be careful because developing a relationship with your constituents is different than developing a relationship with GOD. GOD will always be with you and loves you unconditionally. Remember your constituents who are not for you they are those who are only with you because of what you have. Then after time they leave you when you have nothing else. Your constituents are those people that come in your life to fulfil a purpose and after they fulfil the purpose, they will leave you. People that are for you are those that are with you in your good and bad days, those are the people who are there until the end. The ones you can trust.

Character shows who we are and how committed we are to Christ. Character can be good or bad just like the days we live. Our character can be noticed by the way we express ourselves around other Christians. Treat others the same way you wish to be treated, and above all remember that mutual respect is important. You will be mistreated sometimes remember Jesus was mistreated for no reason at all. We must remain humble and keep a spiritual mind set. This will give you the motivation and strength to go that extra mile. We have those days that take away your winning attitude and days when it is hard to balance your business and personal life. Remember all that GOD has already blessed you and believe he will do it again. When you stumble and lose your way remember that doesn't mean it is over. You may feel alone and like everything is not supposed to turn out this way. You may feel that the more you pray the harder things in life become. Remember that we must be patient enough that we don't give up on what we are waiting for GOD to do. We need to strive to be more like Jesus each day and we will improve our character. We sometimes struggle to be efficient, and sometimes we call on everyone except Jesus. You try to depend on other people and you still run into a wall. Some things in life are too big for us to move so we must pray to Jesus for strength and support. We work so very hard on our jobs and education, but we still forget about Jesus. When the morning starts off bad and your day seems to get worse call on Jesus. Jesus makes the situation better and brightens up the day. You feel like throwing in the towel. GOD wants you to keep on moving and have faith. The season will soon change, and you will not only be efficient, but you will be greatly blessed. So, continue to praise the Lord and you will continue to receive blessings. Have fun but be obedient and serve the Lord. What do you do when it feels like everything you do is a disappointment? What do you do when you feel that prayer is not helping your situation? You stand firm and keep the faith because Jesus is always on time. When you plan make sure you remember to pray. Praying before something happens shows just how strong your faith is in GOD. Some decisions we make in life are too big for us to make. We think we have the answer, but we are really taken a chance. Life is about choices we make, and we must pray that we make the correct choice. A choice is like having two paths to travel in life. For example, a doctor who decides to take the path to the left may end up becoming a successful doctor with no kids and wife. If the same doctor decides to take the path to the right, he may not have become a doctor. He could have become a soldier in the military with two kids and a wife. We must rely on GOD to make the right choice for us. Decisions are very important and the wrong one can change your life forever. When we are young, we make decisions concerning life. We are still learning about life and we seek answers from everyone except GOD. We must be careful of being shy, unmotivated, and discouraged about our decisions. When we choose not to speak up or make the right decision, we can lose someone or something.

We live in a world full of chaos and disappointments. We can only sometimes hope for the best. Men are being stereotyped daily for reasons such as where they come from or what area they grew up in as a child. Sometimes young men must deal with the past their family left or the impression their family left on people. For example, a young man ran into a beautiful female on a Saturday evening in a nearby park. The boy was raised by his mother and father in the church and was a straight "A" student in high school. The parents were making a good living in lower Alabama. The mother came into the father's life and changed a lot of his negative ways. She showed him the beauty of life and that threw GOD everything was possible. Before the change the father had a reputation that was known to be bad by so many people throughout the town. He didn't bother anyone, and he didn't let anyone run over him either. The beautiful female liked the young man and thought he was a gentleman. Weeks went by and the two talked on the telephone each night. The more they talked the more they saw they had in common. They both had birthdays in December, both were sixteen years old, both were workers in the church, and they both loved football. The boy was a good running back and the girl was a cheerleader. As time went by, they began to grow closer together. The young man had not met the parents yet and he had never been to the young ladies' house. They would meet up at the theater or restaurant of her choice. After going on five dates with the young man she decided to invite him over to see her parents.

Her parents were very religious and farmed for a living. The family was indeed excited about seeing this new young man that had captured the eyes of their daughter. When the young man arrived the father of the young lady asked who his folks were. So, the young man told who his father was. Afterwards the young lady's father whole attitude changed. He said to the young man I knew your father and by the way my daughter is not taking company. So please excuse yourself from my house and never come around here again. The young man was very confused because he knew nothing of his father's past. The young daughter was told to never talk to him again. She was very noble and always did what her parents said and although she was in love, she still ended the relationship with the young boy. As time went by the young man continued developing his manhood. He pursued college and continued to play football. The young man became an NFL football player. He was drafted in the first round. Then one summer the young man was visiting home around the fourth of July and he saw the father of the young beautiful girl in the barber shop. However, the boy didn't recognize the beautiful girl's father because it had been so many years. The father sits down while the barber who had been the boys barber his whole childhood begins to gossip. The barber finished cutting his hair after they reminisced on the past. The father was listening then the barber said to the young man that he was very proud of him and his accomplishments. The young man gave the barber his autograph. The haircut was finally over, and the young man tipped the barber a fifty-dollar bill. The barber smiled and gave the young man firm handshake and said goodbye. The father of the young lady who watched impatiently said "who is that man, I heard you say he was from this town". The barber smiled and told the man the boy's mother and fathers name. Then the father of the young girl says I never knew the mother, but I went to school with the father, and he was nothing but trouble. Then the barber smiled and said, "you see you can't always judge the book by its cover." What the barber meant was that just because the father left bad impressions don't count the younger generation out. The young man had time over the years to develop his manhood.

Heavenly Father from the clouds above

Thank you for your grace and mercy,

Your strong everlasting love.

keeps us covered from the enemy.

As we continue our journey you see

We will face obstacles as women and men,

Only by keeping our faith in thee

Amen.

Printed in the United States
By Bookmasters